Biofuels 101: Turning Waste into Energy

Contents

Preface

Introduction

Chapter 1: Introduction to Biofuels

Chapter 2: Types of Biofuels

Chapter 3: How Biofuels are Produced

Chapter 4: Advantages of Biofuels

Chapter 5: Challenges Facing Biofuels

Chapter 6: Biofuels from Waste: Turning Garbage into Energy

Chapter 7: The Future of Biofuels

Chapter 8: Environmental and Economic Impact of Biofuels

Chapter 9: Policy and Regulations Supporting Biofuels

Chapter 10: Conclusion: Can Biofuels Power a Sustainable Future?

Glossary

Preface

As the global demand for sustainable energy sources intensifies, biofuels are emerging as a viable solution for reducing reliance on fossil fuels and transforming waste into energy. The potential of biofuels to turn organic waste into usable energy represents a critical step forward in the transition to a more sustainable and carbon-neutral world. This book, *Biofuels 101: Turning Waste into Energy*, is designed to provide a comprehensive introduction to the role of biofuels in the modern energy landscape.

Part of the Gosships Learning Series, this book offers foundational knowledge for industry professionals, energy managers, policymakers, and students seeking to understand the production, application, and benefits of biofuels. It covers the basics of biofuel types, their production processes, economic considerations, and the regulatory frameworks that govern their use. By combining practical insights with real-world case studies, this book prepares readers to engage with biofuels as a sustainable energy alternative.

The Gosships Learning Series is crafted to provide practical, accessible, and industry-relevant knowledge that supports professional growth. Upon completing this book, you will be able to take an assessment and earn a certificate of achievement, validating your understanding of biofuels and their potential to transform the energy industry.

Introduction

Welcome to *Biofuels 101: Turning Waste into Energy*, a part of the Gosships Learning Series, aimed at providing a clear and concise understanding of how biofuels are shaping the future of energy. This book delves into the science, economics, and practical applications of biofuels, with a focus on how organic waste can be converted into a clean, renewable energy source.

In this book, we explore the following key topics:

- **What Are Biofuels?**: An overview of biofuels, their history, and their potential as a renewable energy source.

- **Biofuel Production Processes**: A detailed look at the methods used to convert biomass and organic waste into usable fuels.

- **Waste as a Resource**: Learn how organic waste from agriculture, industry, and households is being transformed into energy.

- **Economic and Environmental Benefits**: Explore the financial viability of biofuels and their impact on reducing carbon emissions and waste.

- **Regulatory Landscape**: Understand the policies and regulations that promote or hinder biofuel development around the world.

After completing this book, you will have the opportunity to test your knowledge through a certification exam. By passing this exam, you will earn a Certificate of Achievement from the Gosships Learning Series, showcasing your expertise in the field of biofuels.

Who is this book for?

This book is designed for:

- Energy professionals seeking to deepen their understanding of renewable energy options.

- Industrial and agricultural managers looking to turn waste into a valuable energy resource.
- Students and aspiring professionals eager to learn about sustainable energy solutions.
- Policymakers and regulatory bodies involved in the promotion and regulation of biofuels.

By mastering the concepts outlined in this book, you will be equipped to contribute to the development of biofuels and explore innovative solutions for turning waste into energy, making a meaningful impact on the energy industry.

Gosships Learning Series 2024/2025

1. Hydrogen: The Fuel of the Future
2. Green Ammonia: The Next Big Thing in Shipping
3. Decarbonizing Shipping: Pathways to Zero Emissions
4. Battery Technology for Industrial Applications
5. Carbon Capture and Storage: Can It Save the Planet?
6. Biofuels 101: Turning Waste into Energy
7. Understanding LNG (Liquefied Natural Gas)
8. Methanol as a Marine Fuel
9. Offshore Wind Energy: The Future of Renewable Power
10. Tidal and Wave Energy: Harnessing the Ocean
11. Electrofuels: The Next Generation of Carbon-Neutral Fuels
12. Energy Storage Systems for Grid Reliability
13. Hydrogen Fuel Cells for Transportation
14. Solar Energy Innovations: Beyond Solar Panels
15. Smart Grids: The Backbone of Future Energy Systems
16. Ammonia-Hydrogen Blends: A Dual Fuel Solution?
17. Nuclear Power: Small Modular Reactors for a Low-Carbon Future
18. Hydropower: The Oldest Renewable Energy Source
19. Decentralized Energy Systems: Microgrids for Resilience
20. Energy Efficiency Technologies for Industry
21. Hydrogen Production from Seawater
22. Fuel Cells for Maritime Applications
23. Geothermal Energy: Unlocking Earth's Heat
24. Future of EV Charging Infrastructure

25. Synthetic Fuels: Bridging the Gap to Decarbonization
26. Cybersecurity for Maritime and Offshore Operations
27. AI and Automation in Shipping and Logistics
28. Digital Twins in Maritime: Revolutionizing Asset Management
29. Risk Management in Offshore and Maritime Operations
30. Compliance with IMO 2020 Regulations
31. Sustainable Ship Design: Reducing Environmental Impact
32. Marine Renewable Energy: Wave, Tidal, and Offshore Wind Integration
33. Ballast Water Management Systems
34. Blockchain Technology in Shipping: Improving Transparency & Efficiency
35. Effective Supply Chain Management for Energy Industries
36. Leadership in the Energy Transition
37. Effective Crisis Management in Maritime Operations
38. Shipyard Safety Management Systems
39. Port State Control (PSC) Inspection Readiness
40. Remote Vessel Operations and Autonomous Shipping
41. Optimizing Fleet Performance with Data Analytics
42. Maritime Environmental Regulations: Staying Ahead of Compliance
43. Advanced Maintenance Strategies: Condition Monitoring & Predictive Maintenance
44. Global LNG Market: Trends and Opportunities
45. Incident Investigation in Maritime Operations
46. International Maritime Law: Key Concepts and Applications
47. Emergency Preparedness and Response for Offshore Oil & Gas

48. Energy Transition Strategies for Oil and Gas Companies

49. Maritime Drones: Applications and Safety Considerations

50. Effective Project Management in Offshore Energy Projects

All Rights Reserved Disclaimer

The contents of this book, including but not limited to all text, graphics, images, logos, and designs, are the intellectual property of Gosships LLC and are protected by copyright law. No part of this publication may be reproduced, distributed, transmitted, displayed, or modified in any form or by any means, including photocopying, recording, or other electronic or mechanical methods, without the prior written permission of the publisher, except in the case of brief quotations in critical reviews or articles.

The information contained within this book is for educational purposes only and is provided "as is" without warranty of any kind, either expressed or implied. The authors and publishers disclaim any liability for any direct, indirect, or consequential loss or damage arising from the use of the material in this book.

For permissions or inquiries, please contact: admin@gosships.com

© 2024 Gosships LLC. All rights reserved.

Chapter 1

Introduction to Biofuels

As the world grapples with the urgent need to reduce greenhouse gas emissions and transition to sustainable energy sources, biofuels have emerged as a promising solution. **Biofuels** are renewable energy sources derived from organic materials—plants, algae, or waste. Unlike fossil fuels, which take millions of years to form, biofuels can be produced relatively quickly and are considered renewable because the raw materials used to make them can be replenished.

Biofuels are part of a broader strategy to shift away from fossil fuels like coal, oil, and natural gas, which are major contributors to climate change. By converting organic waste into energy, biofuels offer a sustainable alternative that reduces carbon emissions, supports energy security, and makes use of materials that would otherwise end up in landfills.

In this book, we will explore the different types of biofuels, how they are produced, the environmental and economic benefits they offer, and the challenges they face. We'll also look into how waste materials, like agricultural residues and municipal solid waste, can be transformed into valuable energy sources, helping to tackle both energy and waste management challenges at once.

Chapter 2
Types of Biofuels

Biofuels are categorized into three main generations, each with distinct sources and processes.

First-Generation Biofuels

First-generation biofuels are made from food crops such as corn, sugarcane, and soybeans. Ethanol and biodiesel are the two most common first-generation biofuels. Ethanol, usually made from corn or sugarcane, is blended with gasoline to reduce emissions, while biodiesel, made from vegetable oils or animal fats, can be used in diesel engines.

Although first-generation biofuels help reduce emissions compared to fossil fuels, they have sparked controversy. The **food vs. fuel** debate arises because these biofuels compete with food production, potentially driving up food prices and leading to deforestation as more land is used for crops.

Second-Generation Biofuels

Second-generation biofuels address many of the concerns associated with first-generation biofuels. They are derived from **non-food** feedstocks, including agricultural waste, wood chips, and other organic materials like municipal solid waste. Cellulosic ethanol, produced from the fibrous parts of plants, is an example of a second-generation biofuel. These biofuels use materials that would otherwise be discarded, turning waste into energy.

Second-generation biofuels offer several advantages, including a lower impact on food supply and the ability to recycle waste materials. However, the production processes are often more complex and costly than first-generation biofuels.

Third-Generation Biofuels

Third-generation biofuels are produced from **algae** and other microorganisms. Algae can produce biofuels such as biodiesel and bioethanol with fewer land and water requirements than traditional crops. Algae can grow rapidly and can be cultivated on non-arable land, making them a promising biofuel source with less competition for food resources.

The main advantage of third-generation biofuels is their potential for high energy yield and lower environmental impact. However, the technology for large-scale production is still in development, and cost-effective methods for growing and processing algae are needed before third-generation biofuels can become a widespread energy source.

Chapter 3

How Biofuels are Produced

The production of biofuels involves several processes depending on the type of feedstock used. Here are the main methods for producing biofuels.

Fermentation (for Ethanol Production)

Fermentation is the process of converting sugars and starches into ethanol, a type of biofuel. First-generation biofuels like ethanol are typically made from crops like corn or sugarcane. The sugars in these plants are fermented by microorganisms, which produce ethanol as a byproduct. This ethanol is then distilled and purified for use as a fuel, often blended with gasoline.

Transesterification (for Biodiesel Production)

Biodiesel is produced through a process called **transesterification**, which involves reacting vegetable oils or animal fats with alcohol (usually methanol) in the presence of a catalyst. This reaction produces biodiesel and glycerin as a byproduct. Biodiesel can be used directly in diesel engines or blended with petroleum-based diesel.

Anaerobic Digestion (for Biogas Production)

Anaerobic digestion is the process by which organic waste, such as agricultural residues, food waste, or animal manure, is broken down by bacteria in the absence of oxygen. This process produces **biogas**, a mixture of methane and carbon dioxide, which can be used to generate electricity, heat, or fuel vehicles.

Algal Cultivation

Algae can produce biofuels in a variety of ways, depending on the type of algae and the production process. One common method is to grow algae in ponds or bioreactors, harvest the algae, and extract the oils from the cells. These oils can then be converted into biodiesel or other biofuels. Some algae strains can also produce ethanol or hydrogen, making them versatile biofuel sources.

Chapter 4

Advantages of Biofuels

Biofuels offer several key benefits compared to traditional fossil fuels:

Reducing Greenhouse Gas Emissions

Biofuels are considered carbon-neutral because the CO_2 they release when burned is offset by the CO_2 absorbed by the plants used to make them. This is a significant advantage over fossil fuels, which release carbon that has been stored underground for millions of years, contributing to climate change.

Promoting Energy Security

Biofuels can be produced domestically, reducing dependence on foreign oil. This can improve energy security by diversifying the energy supply and creating local jobs in biofuel production and distribution.

Utilizing Waste

Second- and third-generation biofuels, in particular, make use of materials that would otherwise go to waste. By turning agricultural residues, food waste, and municipal solid waste into energy, biofuels help reduce landfill use and lower the environmental impact of waste disposal.

Economic Development

Biofuels can provide new revenue streams for farmers and rural communities by creating demand for crops and agricultural byproducts. Additionally, biofuel production facilities can bring jobs and investment to rural areas, contributing to local economic development.

Chapter 5

Challenges Facing Biofuels

While biofuels have many advantages, they also face several challenges that need to be addressed.

Food vs. Fuel Debate

One of the biggest criticisms of first-generation biofuels is that they use food crops for fuel, which can drive up food prices and lead to food shortages, especially in developing countries. There is also concern that expanding biofuel crop production could lead to deforestation and loss of biodiversity as land is cleared for agriculture.

Land Use and Deforestation

The production of biofuel crops can require large amounts of land and water, which raises concerns about land use and environmental degradation. In some cases, forests are cleared to make room for biofuel crops, releasing carbon stored in trees and soils, which can offset the benefits of biofuels.

Energy Intensity and Production Costs

Producing biofuels, especially second- and third-generation biofuels, can be energy-intensive and expensive. The processes required to convert waste materials or algae into fuel often require significant energy inputs, making it difficult for biofuels to compete with fossil fuels on price.

Scalability and Infrastructure

Scaling up biofuel production to meet global energy demand is a major challenge. In addition, the infrastructure for distributing biofuels, such as fueling stations and pipelines, is not as developed as the infrastructure for fossil fuels. Investment in biofuel infrastructure is needed to support widespread adoption.

Chapter 6

Biofuels from Waste: Turning Garbage into Energy

Second-generation biofuels are made from waste materials that would otherwise be discarded, making them a more sustainable alternative to first-generation biofuels. These waste materials include agricultural residues, wood chips, food waste, and municipal solid waste.

Agricultural Residues

Agricultural waste, such as corn stalks, wheat straw, and rice husks, can be used to produce biofuels. These materials are rich in cellulose, which can be converted into ethanol through fermentation or used to produce biogas through anaerobic digestion.

Municipal Solid Waste

Municipal solid waste, which includes food scraps, paper, and yard waste, can also be converted into biofuels. This process not only generates energy but also reduces the amount of waste sent to landfills. For example, waste-to-energy plants use anaerobic digestion to convert organic waste into biogas, which can be used to generate electricity or fuel vehicles.

Environmental Benefits

Using waste materials to produce biofuels has several environmental benefits. It reduces the amount of waste going to landfills, lowers greenhouse gas emissions, and decreases the reliance on food crops for fuel production. By turning garbage into energy, biofuels contribute to a circular economy, where waste is minimized, and resources are reused.

Chapter 7

The Future of Biofuels

Biofuels have significant potential to play a key role in the global energy transition, especially as technology improves and new feedstocks are developed.

Third-Generation Biofuels and Algae

Algae-based biofuels offer the potential for high energy yields with minimal environmental impact. Algae can grow rapidly in a variety of environments, including on non-arable land and in wastewater, making it an attractive feedstock for future biofuel production. Algae also produce oils that can be converted into biodiesel, and some strains can produce ethanol or hydrogen.

Biofuels and Electric Vehicles

While electric vehicles (EVs) are gaining popularity, biofuels still have an important role to play in reducing emissions from the transportation sector, especially for long-haul trucks, airplanes, and ships, where electrification is more challenging. Biofuels can complement the rise of EVs by providing low-carbon energy for vehicles that are not easily electrified.

Policy and Investment

The future of biofuels will depend largely on government policies and investment. Incentives for biofuel production, such as subsidies and tax credits, can help make biofuels more competitive with fossil fuels. Research and development in advanced biofuels, particularly third-generation biofuels, will also be critical to scaling up production and reducing costs.

Chapter 8

Environmental and Economic Impact of Biofuels

Biofuels offer significant environmental and economic benefits, but there are also risks that need to be managed.

Environmental Benefits

Biofuels reduce greenhouse gas emissions compared to fossil fuels, especially when produced from waste materials or algae. They can also help reduce the environmental impact of waste disposal by turning organic waste into energy. However, the environmental benefits of biofuels depend on how they are produced. For example, biofuels made from food crops or crops grown on deforested land can have a negative impact on the environment.

Economic Benefits

Biofuels can boost rural economies by creating new markets for agricultural products and providing jobs in biofuel production and distribution. In developing countries, biofuels can help reduce dependence on imported fossil fuels, improving energy security and supporting local economic development.

Addressing Environmental Risks

To maximize the environmental benefits of biofuels, it is important to manage the risks associated with land use, water consumption, and biodiversity loss. Sustainable farming practices and the use of non-food feedstocks, such as waste materials or algae, can help mitigate these risks.

Chapter 9

Policy and Regulations Supporting Biofuels

Government policies play a key role in the development and adoption of biofuels. Several countries have implemented policies to support biofuel production and use.

Renewable Fuel Standards

In the United States, the **Renewable Fuel Standard (RFS)** requires a certain percentage of transportation fuels to come from renewable sources, including biofuels. This policy has helped drive the growth of the biofuel industry by creating a guaranteed market for biofuels.

EU's Renewable Energy Directive

In Europe, the **Renewable Energy Directive (RED)** sets targets for the use of renewable energy in transportation, including biofuels. The directive also promotes the use of advanced biofuels made from waste materials and non-food feedstocks.

Incentives and Subsidies

Many governments provide financial incentives for biofuel production, such as subsidies, tax credits, and grants. These incentives help offset the higher production costs of biofuels and encourage investment in biofuel infrastructure and research.

Chapter 10

Conclusion: Can Biofuels Power a Sustainable Future?

Biofuels are an important part of the renewable energy landscape, offering a way to reduce greenhouse gas emissions, promote energy security, and turn waste into energy. However, biofuels are not without their challenges, including the food vs. fuel debate, land use concerns, and high production costs.

As technology advances and new feedstocks are developed, biofuels have the potential to play a larger role in the global energy transition. Second- and third-generation biofuels, in particular, offer a sustainable alternative to fossil fuels by making use of waste materials and algae.

To realize the full potential of biofuels, governments, businesses, and researchers must work together to overcome the challenges facing the industry and scale up production. With the right policies, investments, and technological innovations, biofuels can contribute to a cleaner, more sustainable energy future for the planet.

Glossary - *Biofuels 101: Turning Waste into Energy*:

1. **Advanced Biofuels**: Biofuels made from non-food feedstocks such as agricultural waste, algae, or other sustainable materials.

2. **Anaerobic Digestion**: A process where microorganisms break down organic matter in the absence of oxygen, producing biogas.

3. **Bagasse**: The fibrous residue left after extracting juice from sugarcane, used as a biofuel feedstock.

4. **Biodiesel**: A renewable fuel made from plant oils, animal fats, or recycled cooking oil, used in diesel engines.

5. **Bioenergy**: Energy produced from biological sources such as plants, organic waste, or wood.

6. **Bioethanol**: A form of ethanol produced from biomass, commonly used as an additive to gasoline.

7. **Biogas**: A gaseous fuel produced by the anaerobic digestion of organic matter such as food waste or manure.

8. **Biomass**: Organic material that comes from plants and animals, used as a fuel to produce bioenergy.

9. **Bio-refinery**: A facility that converts biomass into fuels, chemicals, and energy, similar to how an oil refinery processes crude oil.

10. **Biotechnology**: The use of living organisms or systems to develop biofuels or improve biofuel production processes.

11. **Carbon Intensity (CI)**: A measure of the amount of carbon dioxide emissions produced per unit of energy output.

12. **Carbon Neutral**: A process or activity that results in no net release of carbon dioxide into the atmosphere.

13. **Cellulosic Ethanol**: Ethanol produced from cellulose (fibrous plant material) rather than from sugars or starches.

14. **CHP (Combined Heat and Power)**: A system that generates both electricity and useful heat from the same energy source, including biofuels.

15. **Co-firing**: The process of burning biomass alongside fossil fuels in power plants to reduce carbon emissions.

16. **CNG (Compressed Natural Gas)**: A fuel made from methane that is often produced from biogas, used as a cleaner alternative to gasoline or diesel.

17. **Digestate**: The nutrient-rich byproduct of anaerobic digestion, used as a fertilizer.

18. **Drop-in Biofuels**: Biofuels that can directly replace conventional fossil fuels without needing modifications to existing infrastructure.

19. **E10**: A fuel blend consisting of 10% ethanol and 90% gasoline.

20. **E85**: A fuel blend of 85% ethanol and 15% gasoline, used in flexible-fuel vehicles.

21. **Ethanol**: A renewable fuel made from biomass, primarily used as a gasoline additive to reduce emissions.

22. **Feedstock**: Raw materials such as agricultural waste, forest residues, or algae used to produce biofuels.

23. **Fermentation**: A process in which sugars are converted into ethanol by the action of yeast or bacteria.

24. **First-Generation Biofuels**: Biofuels made from food crops like corn or sugarcane, primarily used to produce ethanol or biodiesel.

25. **Flex-Fuel Vehicles (FFVs)**: Vehicles that can run on more than one type of fuel, typically gasoline and ethanol blends.

26. **Glycerol**: A byproduct of biodiesel production, used in various industries such as cosmetics and pharmaceuticals.

27. **Greenhouse Gas (GHG)**: Gases like CO_2 and methane that trap heat in the Earth's atmosphere, contributing to climate change.

28. **HVO (Hydrotreated Vegetable Oil)**: A high-quality renewable diesel made from vegetable oils or animal fats using hydrogenation technology.

29. **Hydrolysis**: A chemical process that breaks down cellulose or starches into simple sugars for biofuel production.

30. **Jatropha**: A drought-resistant plant whose seeds contain oil that can be converted into biodiesel.

31. **LCA (Life Cycle Assessment)**: A method to assess the environmental impacts of a product, including biofuels, throughout its entire lifecycle.

32. **Lignocellulose**: A complex structure of plant biomass made up of cellulose, hemicellulose, and lignin, used in the production of cellulosic biofuels.

33. **Methane (CH_4)**: A potent greenhouse gas that is also the primary component of biogas and natural gas.

34. **Microalgae**: Single-celled algae used as a feedstock for biofuel production, particularly for biodiesel and biojet fuel.

35. **MTBE (Methyl Tertiary-Butyl Ether)**: A gasoline additive that is being replaced by bioethanol due to environmental concerns.

36. **Palm Oil**: An edible oil used in the production of biodiesel, though its use is controversial due to environmental concerns.

37. **Renewable Diesel**: A fuel made from renewable resources such as vegetable oils, animal fats, and waste oils, chemically similar to petroleum diesel.

38. **Renewable Energy Directive (RED II)**: An EU policy that sets targets for the use of renewable energy, including biofuels.

39. **Renewable Identification Numbers (RINs)**: Credits used to track renewable fuel production and compliance with U.S. renewable fuel standards.

40. **Second-Generation Biofuels**: Biofuels made from non-food feedstocks such as agricultural residues, grasses, or waste materials.

41. **Starch-Based Ethanol**: Ethanol produced from the fermentation of starches found in crops like corn or wheat.

42. **Syngas (Synthesis Gas)**: A gas mixture of hydrogen, carbon monoxide, and carbon dioxide, used as an intermediate in the production of biofuels.

43. **Third-Generation Biofuels**: Biofuels made from algae and other advanced feedstocks that do not compete with food crops.

44. **Transesterification**: The chemical process used to convert oils or fats into biodiesel and glycerol.

45. **Vegetable Oil**: A feedstock used for producing biodiesel, obtained from crops like soybeans, canola, or palm.

46. **Waste-to-Energy (WtE)**: A process that converts waste materials into energy, including biofuels derived from organic waste.

47. **Wood Pellets**: Compressed biomass fuel made from wood waste, used in power plants and heating systems.

48. **Xylose**: A sugar derived from hemicellulose in plants, used in the production of biofuels.

49. **Yeast**: Microorganisms used in the fermentation process to convert sugars into ethanol for biofuel production.

50. **Zymomonas mobilis**: A type of bacterium used in bioethanol production due to its efficient fermentation process.